THE 180°
DEVOTIONAL

THE 180°
DEVOTIONAL

SHELDON NEIL

CONCLUSIO
HOUSE PUBLISHING

"The 180° Devotional"
REL012020 RELIGION/Christian Life/Devotional
REL012120 RELIGION/Christian Life/Spiritual Growth

Printed in Canada
First Printing, 2017

ISBN 978-1-988847-01-6

Edited by Kerri-Ann Haye-Donawa

Published by:
Conclusio House Publishing
Brampton, Ontario
Canada
www.conclusiohouse.com

I dedicate this devotional book to my beautiful wife, Alicia, and my daughter, Reigan-Sijourney, a.k.a. "Brilliant!"
God, I give you all the glory for what you have spoken through the pages of this book.
Thank you for your Word.

FOREWORD

I believe one of the greatest desires of God the Father is not only to have a relationship with you, through Jesus Christ, but also for you to step into the purpose He has invented for your life. Jeremiah 1:5 says, "Before I formed you in the womb I knew you, and before you were born I consecrated you; I appointed you a prophet to the nations." As He was creating you and me, He had a purpose in mind for us. He is an intentional God, who created all things with a purpose.

When you come into relationship with God, you start to realize that there is more. I believe that the more we seek Him is the more He will begin to unfold His master plan for our lives. Proverbs 3:5-6 (NLT) says, "Trust in the Lord with all your heart; do not depend on your own understanding. Seek His will in all you do, and He will show you which path to take."

How do we know we are fulfilling God's purpose for our lives? Know that it is a lifelong pursuit to be in, and to stay in, the centre of the purpose for your life. "Don't copy the behaviour and customs of this world, but let God transform you into a new person by changing the way you think. Then you will learn to know God's will for you, which is good and pleasing and perfect" (Romans 12:2 NLT). Allow God to transform you into the person He is calling you to be, and watch Him show you more and more of His purpose for you.

One of the things I advise everyone is to stand on His promises. As you are searching for purpose in your life, declare over yourself what the psalmist wrote: "The Lord will fulfill His purpose for me" (Psalm 138:8a NRSV). Decree it over your life, and watch how God reveals His will to you.

My prayer is that through this devotional you will be challenged, each day, to seek and step into the purpose God has for your life. You will find much fulfillment, joy, and completion, knowing that this is what you were created to do.

I've known Sheldon Neil for several years. I've watched him and all the things that God has been doing through his life. If there is anyone I know that is moving and operating in purpose, it is my friend Sheldon Neil. And I know that this is just the beginning.

Phil Galindo
Youth Pastor
The Potter's House North Dallas
Pastor Sheryl Brady (Lead Pastor)
Presiding Prelate T.D. Jakes

TABLE OF CONTENTS

INTRODUCTION

Since I was a child, I've always been sensitive to the voice and move of God in my life. I'm not sure if that kind of thing is directly inherited or picked up by other means, but growing up, my mother was always someone with a strong sense of discernment. It was almost comical; there was nothing you could get by her. You couldn't trick her. It was as if she would see something coming before it happened. If I thought of secretly stealing and eating some freshly baked cookies, she'd say to me before they were even finished baking, "Don't think about eating them just yet." That kind of thing. Anyway, I digress.

As early as I can remember, I've always been sensitive to the unseen world. This sensitivity equipped me with a certain acute awareness and consciousness of the spiritual—both good and bad. One thing I've learned is that God has a pre-ordained plan for our lives. This is such an exciting thing to know. God wants you and me to succeed. The God of the universe wants you and me to live the best life we can.

But the story doesn't end there. There is another side to this. There is an enemy out there with another plan in mind. Dark spiritual forces exist to viciously, and without prejudice, stop the plan of God from manifesting in our lives. These dark forces are demons, who, in short, carry out the plan of Satan. The Bible categorizes Satan and his forces into one group known as the kingdom of darkness. It goes a little further to reveal their game plan in John 10:10, by saying they seek to "steal, kill, and destroy." These forces work to frustrate, delay, and, ultimately, stop us from walking in the plan of God for our lives. They may exact their influence through people, life situations, or other means. Any way they can get to us, they will try—that boss that seems to have it out for you, that abusive relationship, that addiction that sometimes seems impossible to break. Any way they can.

The Book of Ephesians shows us how our lives intersect with this dark kingdom. Ephesians 6:12 (NIV) says, *"For our struggle is not against flesh and blood, but against the rulers, against the authorities, against the powers of this dark world and against the spiritual forces of evil in the heavenly realms."*

One major way that I've seen the kingdom of darkness rob countless people from experiencing everything God has for them is by shrouding their ability to know God's plan and purpose for their lives. No matter their political stripe, religious background, culture, or creed, there is a central question people around the world continue to ask: Why am I here? What is my purpose? The sad thing is that many go through life, well into their old age, sometimes even into death without truly knowing why they lived.

I'm here to let you know that it is impossible to discover your purpose in life without God. Only He holds the answer to why you continue to open your eyes every morning and continue to exist day after day, year after year. No self-help book or self-help conference has the answer. Only God.

On the road to unlocking your purpose, the devil and his forces will try to stop the revelation from hitting your life. I want to let you know that as soon as you ask God to reveal your purpose, He will. But the devil will send situations to distract you and get you off track. Sometimes the war takes place in the spirit world. It happened to Daniel.

Daniel 10 tells the story. Daniel prayed to receive revelation concerning Israel, but the angel released to bring the revelation and insight concerning Israel's future was delayed for twenty-one days by a dark spiritual force known as the Prince of Persia. This powerful demonic force worked to try and stop the revelation from reaching Daniel. In fact, the angel carrying Daniel's answer contended with the demonic force. Things got so intense that the heavenly archangel Michael came to help and, ultimately, the angel of the Lord carrying Daniel's answer proceeded. But, for twenty-one days, a real battle was going on.

This devotional is designed to help you unlock your purpose in life. The passages are designed to equip you to unlock every chain the enemy may have attached to your path in life, and empower you to make a 180-degree turn and go in the opposite direction, toward victory. The passages have been carefully and purposefully put together for a twenty-one-day experience. Each passage is designed to bring a precise breakthrough over any force assigned to hold up your blessing or the answer of God from manifesting in your life. These passages are designed to break every dark, princely chain over your life. Don't continue existing on a road of depression, defeat, worry, doubt, or whatever path the enemy might have laid for you. It's time to make a 180-degree turn and proceed on the path God has laid for you. Every locked door, held up by the enemy, is about to be unlocked. You are about to walk on a path of victory, success, and purpose.

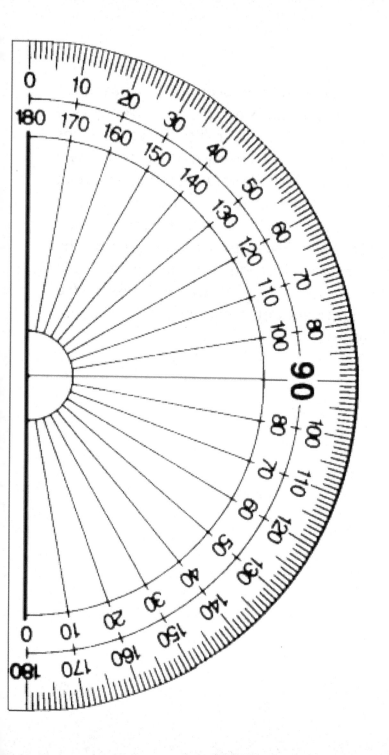

LIVING OUT LOUD

"For I know the plans I have for you. Plans to
give you hope and a beautiful future."
(Jeremiah 29:11)

I remember it like it was yesterday—riding my bike as a child through unknown streets, wooded areas, and reaching the big moment. "What's the big moment?" you may be asking. I'm talking about when you reach the fork in the road, and must decide which way to go. *Should I go right? Take the centre road? Or should I go left?* Each road has an adventure, and they all look good. But which one is the right one for me?

For many, this is what life looks like, especially when it comes to living life out loud. Again, I can hear you asking, "What in the world does *living out loud* mean?" Living out loud is existing without a glass ceiling over your life. It is existing without hindrances or borders that function to box you in from living a fulfilled life. Sounds too good to be true? It isn't.

I've discovered that the ability to live life to the fullest, free of hindrances and shortcomings, rests on one major key—being connected to *the way* of the Lord. When I live my life God's way, I find my destiny, my future, and, ultimately, the freedom that will enable me to be all God has created me to be.

We live in a world that points us in different directions. Just like those afternoon bike rides as a child, each direction promises us adventure and seemingly the best existence. We encounter it every day. Do you want to lose twelve pounds by Christmas? Try *this way*. 24-hour abs? Try working out *this way*. Need twelve easy steps to grow your business? Grow it *this way*. The trappings of life tend to put us on a road to experiencing the world around us.

Don't get me wrong. Not all self-help books, workout techniques, and growth strategies are wrong, although I am still searching to find a "24-hour abs" system that will work for me. But I'm willing to bet you that pretty much every road this busy life throws your way leaves you feeling unsatisfied. Every manmade road leaves us as consumers, experiencing and wanting more because we are unsatisfied. The point is how many "breakthroughs" can there be, especially when each new "breakthrough" is supposed to trump the video that preceded it? In the often hurried, crazy, busy, and overly informed world we live in, we need to ensure that our lives are connected, above all, to the greatest *way* we can ever journey on—God's way. He has a foolproof plan for our lives. Any life existence outside of that will leave us feeling unfulfilled. And an unfulfilled life is never lived out loud.

Jeremiah 29:11 says, *"For I know the plans I have for you,"* declares the Lord, *"plans to prosper you and not to harm you, plans to give you hope and a future."* The plans or way God has for us points to a life fulfilled. Society has a way of teaching us to take hold of our life and direct it in the way we think it should go. In a way, I agree. In that, we should each take responsibility for going after our dreams and unearthing the destiny that is within us. But how can we take control of something that isn't up to us? Proverbs 19:21 (NIV) says, *"Many are the plans in a person's heart, but it is the LORD's purpose that prevails."* In other words, we can make, and are encouraged to make, as many plans as we can for our lives, but we must never forget that there is a master-architect who has prescribed a way for us to walk. He has a wonderful road waiting for us. And the invitation of Scripture is to say in submission, "God, whatever your way is for my life, I want to walk in it, because I know whatever you have planned for me is going to be good."

Devotional Prayer

Lord, what is the way that you've ordained for me to take this day? Reveal it to me. I know it is good. I know it is the best for me. I know it is blessed. I'm ready to walk in the steps you've laid out. Amen.

180° KEYS
SCRIPTURES FOR MEDITATION

Ephesians 2:10:

"For we are God's handiwork, created in Christ Jesus to do good works, which God prepared in advance for us to do."

Philippians 1:6:

"Being confident of this, that he who began a good work in you will carry it on to completion until the day of Christ Jesus."

2 Corinthians 5:7:

"For we live by faith, not by sight."

Proverbs 3:5-6:

"Trust in the LORD with all your heart and lean not on your own understanding; in all your ways submit to him, and he will make your paths straight."

NOTES:

God has a plan and purpose for my life, which I feel I'm walking in right now. But I desire to finish strong and in that God's purposes for me need to come through prayer. Jesus what are the things you have before me & what me to do now & in the future - create me to good works to glorify Jesus - He want me to fulfill my gifts for His Kingdom.

THIS THING CALLED PURPOSE

"For he chose us in him before the creation of the world to be holy and blameless in his sight. In love." (Ephesians 1:4 NIV)

I've worked in television as a host and producer for almost a decade. I've interviewed stars, popular authors, politicians, and other notable individuals. However, some of the most riveting interviews I've done have tackled some of life's biggest questions. Perhaps the most well-known for many is, "What is my purpose for living?"

I've discovered that finding one's purpose in life is a gift. I use the word gift because there are millions of people roaming this earth who are living, but who have no sense of direction. Those who can wake up in the morning and have the slightest sense of why they exist have received a precious gift.

It is easy to chase after the "gift" that is

discovering one's purpose; however, if we are not careful, this chase can leave us feeling exhausted, stressed out, and depressed. Can you imagine living a life trying to find your purpose, and you end up progressively more depressed? That is no way to live.

I want to submit to you that the purpose for your life isn't found in searching for it, but rather in coming into relationship with He who holds your purpose. Let me put it this way: your purpose isn't found in *the thing* but rather in *the giver* of the thing. Who is the giver of purpose? That, my friend, is God the Father.

Purpose is God's decided agenda for your life. I've personally found that as you age, many people will offer their analysis of why, they think, you exist. In most cases, it is good natured. People may see you excel in a certain discipline or talent, and immediately conclude that is the purpose for your life. But we can't equate talent with purpose. Furthermore, if we are not careful, it is easy to believe what people say, and attribute to our life a purpose and direction that was never for us to begin with.

Luke 1:26–38 outlines the orchestration of purpose for us. It is the story of Gabriel appearing to Mary, announcing Jesus' birth. Let's take a look.

"And behold, thou shalt conceive in thy womb, and bring forth a son, and shalt call his name Jesus." (v. 31) Before we go further, it is important to know that in early Jewish tradition, parents would not just give their child a name without giving it serious thought. They believed a child's name represented its character and the kind of person that child would become. So what does the name Jesus mean? Scholars will tell you that it means God delivers or saves. Let's go a step further.

"He shall be great, and shall be called the Son of the Highest: and the Lord God shall give unto him the throne of his father David. And he shall reign over the house of Jacob forever; and of his kingdom there shall be no end." (vv. 32–33)

The words used to describe Jesus weren't simply descriptors of a person's life; rather, God was revealing His decided agenda for Jesus' life. He was literally showing Mary the type of life Jesus was going to display, and the impact His life would have.

God knows the path you should take. He knows what He has created you for. God knows it. The enemy wants us to spend years running after the *it* we think it is, and totally step over the source that actually unlocks and reveals it. We will never find purpose outside of finding God first.

Devotional Prayer

Father, I ask you to reveal to me what your decided agenda is for my life. I'm seeking you first, because I know when I put you first, everything else will easily follow. I trust you, and I'm excited for what is ahead. Amen.

God has chosen a
path for us, but
the enemy want to
misdirect us, got us
Chasing the wrong thy.

180° KEYS
SCRIPTURES FOR MEDITATION

Exodus 9:16:

"But I have raised you up for this very purpose, that I might show you my power and that my name might be proclaimed in all the earth."

Romans 8:28:

"And we know that in all things God works for the good of those who love him, who have been called according to his purpose."

Ephesians 3:20–21:

"Now to him who is able to do immeasurably more than all we ask or imagine, according to his power that is at work within us, to him be glory in the church and in Christ Jesus throughout all generations, for ever and ever! Amen."

Ecclesiastes 3:1:

"There is a time for everything, and a season for every activity under the heavens"

NOTES:

Even when things go

wrong... or like, or we

do something where we

might have gotten off

track and did things

because we thought they

were right, or did

them for our benefit

we can use them to

check in on life, to

use them for good.

Life, over time will

straighten out, to do the

work and growth that!

THE PRESSURE TEST

"No temptation has overtaken you except what is common to mankind. And God is faithful; he will not let you be tempted beyond what you can bear. But when you are tempted, he will also provide a way out so that you can endure it."
(1 Corinthians 10:13 NIV)

No matter your age, status, culture, or religious belief system, everyone deals with temptation. The only difference is found in which of our appetites is pressured.

Perhaps no one faced more intense temptation than the three Hebrew boys. I mean, they faced a tough situation. It was either bow before the golden image of King Nebuchadnezzar or be thrown into a fiery furnace. The temptation to simply bow and forsake their convictions must have been incredibly high, especially in the face of death. But, somehow, they didn't give in. They stayed faithful to God the Father and, more so, to their convictions.

Persevere don't give up!

Oftentimes, for many of us, facing temptation ends with us giving in to the very thing we said we wouldn't. It wasn't until after taking a deeper look at how temptation works that I realized two important keys:

1. Temptation creates pressure.

Temptation is a feeling that is usually accompanied by the conclusion that you must do it. And not doing whatever the "it" is will end with you missing out on something huge. For many, the thought of missing out is enough to get them to jump over the edge. But the Bible encourages us in Romans 12:2 (NIV) not to *"conform to the pattern of this world, but be transformed by the renewing of your mind. Then you will be able to rest and approve what God's will is – his good, pleasing and perfect will."*

You see, to overcome temptation, we must look at every situation through God's eyes. We must weigh every situation we face in life by His perspective. Once we do this, our minds will be immediately renewed. How so? Looking at life's tests God's way helps to give us access to the heart of God and, by extension, the answer of how to react to these tests. If I can renew my mind, I can take the pressure off myself and put it on the source, who knows the end from the beginning. The wisdom of God, which is always rooted in wanting the best for me, will help guide me in taking the next step in the right direction.

2. Temptation is an external test.

Oftentimes, temptation will highlight to you a system or way of thinking that the masses are following, implying that you should follow, too. This can be as simple as a group of friends deciding to go to a place you know you shouldn't go to, but everyone going creates a structure, and that structure inadvertently creates norms, so it is easy to get swept away in it. But we must understand that God did not call His children to fit in.

In fact, Jesus, throughout His earthly ministry, never fit in. He was called names, ostracized, and, ultimately, crucified for going against the religious structure of the day. I know you may feel like a misfit, but always remember that God has made you more than a conqueror. That means nothing can hold you down—no system, societal norm, or click-culture. Therefore, it's not necessary for you to say yes to temptation.

God has something, and has made you, so much bigger than what might be tugging at your heart. You are bigger, because you have a BIG God living on the inside of you.

Devotional Prayer

Father, give me the courage, by your Spirit, to follow your way, and to not give in to temptation. Amen.

180° KEYS
SCRIPTURES FOR MEDITATION

1 Corinthians 10:13:

"No temptation has overtaken you except what is common to mankind. And God is faithful; he will not let you be tempted beyond what you can bear. But when you are tempted, he will also provide a way out so that you can endure it."

Ephesians 6:10:

"Finally, be strong in the Lord and in his mighty power."

1 Peter 5:8:

"Be alert and of sober mind. Your enemy the devil prowls around like a roaring lion looking for someone to devour."

Romans 12:2:

"Do not conform to the pattern of this world, but be transformed by the renewing of your mind. Then you will be able to test and approve what God's will is--his good, pleasing and perfect will."

NOTES:

The followers of Jesus are
never going to fit into
this world, and if they do
they are compromising and
diving into [ ] Jesus has promised
He will always give us a
way out and he gives us
His power

Resisting is a key part to
finding victory in our God!
I need to be constantly
alert.

Temptation, Be Alert
God's power

KEEP IT MOVING

"The ravens brought him bread and meat in the morning and bread and meat in the evening, and he drank from the brook. Some time later the brooks dried because there had been no rain in the land. Then the word of the Lord came to him: "Go at once to Zarephath in the region of Sidon and stay there. I have directed a widow there to supply you with food." (1 Kings 17:6-9 NIV)

One thing Jesus' earthly ministry teaches us is the importance of knowing how to manage time. Time and time again, throughout His ministry, as soon as Jesus finished what He went to do in a town or community, He moved on to the next location. He never stayed longer than intended. Whenever He was pressured by a crowd, instead of revealing the full scope of His coming, He kept it to Himself, knowing that it wasn't the right time to reveal it. The inability to manage time has lifelong consequences. Just think, time wasted can never be recovered. For example, you will never get back last week Monday. Knowing how much of your time and energy you give to a relationship, job, or situation is very important. Let's go a step further.

Understanding time management isn't only about knowing how much time you give to something, but also knowing when it's time to leave that situation, argument, relationship, you name it, and move on. Humans are creatures of habit and comfort. So, it's in our nature to fall into stagnation. However, remaining in a place in life that you have outgrown limits your personal growth of character. Holding on to things that no longer feed you often leads to those things feeding on you. The situation, relationship, or job begins to drain you.

Our immediate and, quite frankly, easiest response is to blame the thing we're connected to. But it might not be the thing we're connected to that's at fault. No, it may just be that we're trying to drink from a source that has dried up. That was Elijah's situation. He was used to being fed by the brook. If he was thirsty, the brook was there. He'd grown accustomed to, and comfortable with, the brook. When the brook dried up, he wasn't ready to move on. But he needed to.

Are you holding on to dry places in your life? Are you trying to extract life from dead situations? It may not be easy, but you must keep it moving. There is a new place in which God wants to use you. A new place in which God wishes you to grow. A new place that God has prepared for you that will launch you to a higher place of growth. Keep it moving.

Devotional Prayer

Father, I ask you to lead me through every situation of life. Be my guiding light. Give me the sensitivity to recognize when it's time to move on from the dry places in my life, and the courage to leave my comfort zone. I'm excited for what is ahead. Amen.

180° KEYS
SCRIPTURES FOR MEDITATION

Philippians 3:13–14:

"Brothers and sisters, I do not consider myself yet to have taken hold of it. But one thing I do: Forgetting what is behind and straining toward what is ahead, I press on toward the goal to win the prize for which God has called me heavenward in Christ Jesus."

Psalm 32:8:

"I will instruct you and teach you in the way you should go; I will counsel you with my loving eye on you."

Philippians 4:13:

"I can do all this through him who gives me strength."

Isaiah 43:18:

"Forget the former things; do not dwell on the past."

NOTES:

While my past can be filled with good things and bad things I must keep moving forward to keep my eyes on Jesus. There are time to move on in life, in relationships, jobs, churches, and following Jesus. Unfortunately we can't move on as quickly or we can't have liked in our relationship with some people.

BELIEVING GOD AT HIS WORD

"Do not fear, for I am with you; do not be dismayed, for I am your God. I will strengthen you and help you; I will uphold you with my righteous right hand." (Isaiah 41:10 NIV)

Do you believe what God tells you? I mean, really believe it? Or is there a space, albeit small, deep within your mind or heart that says, "You know, I'm not sure about this."

I've often found that it is sometimes the seemingly easiest verses to wrap our heads around in Scripture that can be the most challenging to integrate into our daily lives. For example, a verse as simple as Isaiah 41:10, which says, *"Do not fear, for I am with you; do not be dismayed, for I am your God. I will strengthen you and help you; I will uphold you with my righteous right hand."* The promise and reassurance of God

24

toward us is clear in this verse. We don't need to fear; He will sustain us.

No matter what you're facing in life, God says, "Fear not! I am with you." But if we are honest with ourselves, in most cases, when life happens, those two directive words, "fear not," sometimes seem easier said than done. When you're fired from that job; when your bank account balance doesn't read what you think it should; or when the doctor says, "It's cancer," somehow those two simple words, "fear not," seem like a hard pill to swallow.

But I've learned that God's directives don't ask us to ignore the emotions we feel when life happens. You've lost your job? You may feel scared. But with that emotion, fear not. The doctor said it was cancer? You may feel devastated. That's okay. But with that feeling of devastation, fear not. You see, God's directives are there to provide us with strength and encouragement to deal with the emotions and feelings we will face when a trial hits our life. The directives of God were never there for you to ignore the emotions you have when life hits you hard. Rather, they are there to restore you from those emotions back to a place of strength and victory.

When God gives you a promise in His Word, no matter what life may look like, no matter the situations you may face, believe God at His Word. Deuteronomy 31:6 encourages us by saying, *"Be strong and courageous. Do not be afraid or terrified because of them, for the LORD your God goes with you; he will never leave you nor forsake you."* My friends, that is a promise from God. Rest on it. I promise you, you are not alone in this.

Devotional Prayer

Father, increase my faith to trust and believe you at your Word. I put away fear. I put away doubt from my life. Help me to remain steadfast and to depend on you, not matter the situation I face. Amen.

180° KEYS
SCRIPTURES FOR MEDITATION

Deuteronomy 31:6:

"Be strong and courageous. Do not be afraid or terrified because of them, for the LORD your God goes with you; he will never leave you nor forsake you."

Isaiah 26:3:

"You will keep in perfect peace those whose minds are steadfast, because they trust in you."

Isaiah 41:10:

"So do not fear, for I am with you; do not be dismayed, for I am your God. I will strengthen you and help you; I will uphold you with my righteous right hand."

Psalm 34:17:

"The righteous cry out, and the LORD hears them; he delivers them from all their troubles."

NOTES:

God says in His word
He will never forsake us
and either that is true
or not

No matter what I'm
facing in life, whether [us],
sickness, job, family He
says to "FEAR NOT"

I need to meditate
on the scripture that
will strengthen me in
my walk with the
Lord Jesus!

THIS DAY IS MADE FOR YOU!

"This is the day the Lord has made; we will rejoice and be glad in it." (Psalm 118:24 NKJV)

I'm sure you can remember the day. You just finished experiencing the best weekend of your life. I mean, all the makings of a great weekend hit the bull's-eye. Just incredible. Suddenly, you wake up to the annoying sound of an alarm clock. In response, you turn and lay on your back, with your face pointed toward the ceiling. It all sinks in. It's Monday morning.

I think out of all the days of the week, Monday gets the worst treatment. Now, I don't know the statistics, but I bet if you were to take a random poll on your street, asking neighbours which day of the week they hate most, the resounding answer would be Monday. Why? For a lot of people, Monday symbolizes the end of experiencing life the way they want to. It's the end of freedom, pleasure, and, at a deeper level, control. It's the belief that now that Monday is here, we have to plug back into the machine of life that often accompanies an experience no longer driven by our own power but rather rests in the hands of an awful boss, a boring job, or an unfulfilled life.

We've all been there. We face the start of the week, hoping that it will treat us well. We hope and pray that we will make it out the other end. But I believe God wishes for us to think better for our lives. Let's look at our focus scripture. Psalm 118:24 NKJV says, *"This is the day the Lord has made, we will rejoice and be glad in it."*

The phrase "we will rejoice" is declarative and absolute. It is not a suggestion or something hopeful. It is about deciding to speak into existence the day you plan to experience. Let's go a step further. The decision to rejoice does not rest or depend on the success or failures the day may bring. It is saying that despite what may happen, God has orchestrated this day, and I will rejoice and be glad in it. Instead of asking the best for your day and hoping things go well, command the best out of your day and out of yourself.

Our focus verse for today declares that *"This is the day the Lord has made."* Let's establish an important detail. Every day we open our eyes to see, God has not only graced us to see it, but God has also created it. Genesis 1:3–5 (NIV) says, *"And God said, 'Let there be light,' and there was light. God saw that the light was good, and he separated the light from the darkness. God called the light Day, and the darkness he called Night. And there was evening, and there was morning—the first day."*

But check this out: Jeremiah 29:11 (NIV) says, *"For I know the plans I have for you,"* declares the LORD, *"plans to prosper you and not to harm you, plans to give you hope and a future."* That means every day I wake up to see has been made by God for me to win. With that in mind, I cannot help but rejoice and be glad. In fact, no matter what bad report the enemy may try to bring my way during the day, I know it's going to end up working for my good, because God created the day. As a child of God, the day has been made for me to win.

The next time you wake up and are dreading what you think might be a terrible day or week, remember that God has created that day especially for you. And guess what? He's made that day for you to win. So rejoice. Stir up your faith. Be glad!

Devotional Prayer

Father, I thank you for waking me up this morning. I thank you that you've made this day for me to win. I receive the favour, opportunities, and blessings you have in store for me today. I rejoice and praise you in advance. No matter what may come my way today, I thank you that it is working out for my good. Amen.

180° KEYS
SCRIPTURES FOR MEDITATION

Deuteronomy 20:4:

"For the LORD your God is the one who goes with you to fight for you against your enemies to give you victory."

Psalm 3:8:

"From the LORD comes deliverance. May your blessing be on your people."

Romans 8:31-32:

"What, then, shall we say in response to these things? If God is for us, who can be against us? He who did not spare his own Son, but gave him up for us all—how will he not also, along with him, graciously give us all things?"

1 Corinthians 15:57:

"But thanks be to God! He gives us the victory through our Lord Jesus Christ."

NOTES:

the Lord he creator
the sky for me and
I will rejoice.
Thank you every for
up discomzeration my
God give me appitata
to serve him and in
this I will rejoice.
No weapon may prosper
against me.
Thank you Lord for this
day

34

HAVE YOU MADE ROOM?

*"And no one pours new wine into old wineskins...
no, they pour new wine into new wineskins."*
(Mark 2:22 NIV)

My wife and I love decorating. Our favourite channel to watch together is HGTV. In fact, we could binge-watch that channel all day, if the mood struck us right. We love the creativity, the work, and the seeming breath of fresh air that goes into redefining a space. It's awesome. One day, we thought of revamping our living room. I don't like clutter. I'm all about open-concept rooms. We had three couches to move and a table. No matter how many times we shifted the couches and table, we couldn't find the sweet spot. We couldn't find a layout that worked for the room. We tried every configuration we could imagine.

Eventually, we realized that for us to get the configuration and open concept we wanted, we had to move the table out of the room. There were some reservations about the idea, but, ultimately, it was the only way. Once we removed the table from the room, we suddenly found ourselves with plenty of room to create the new environment we were hoping for. The problem wasn't the room itself. We just had to make room for our ideas to come to life.

So many times, God wishes to do something fresh and inspiring in our lives. He desires to push us to the next level of living and experience. But oftentimes, if we're honest with ourselves, we resist change. As humans, we prefer feeling comfortable than uncomfortable. We would rather be certain of our present than uncertain. To some degree, it's understandable. But I've learned that giving room for God to work something new in my life also comes with giving room for me to feel uncomfortable. That discomfort is not rooted in fear or doubt. Rather, it's a space that allows me the opportunity to stretch beyond my comfort zone to discover a new existence. That existence can manifest as new opportunities, a deeper understanding of self, of God, of my wife, of my family, and so much more.

If we go through life without giving ourselves room to expand and spread our wings beyond our comfort zone, we will never come to realize the full measure of our God-given potential and ability. In short, we will live a stunted life, and that's not the way God intended for us to live.

There is so much more that God wants to do in and through your life. You've only scratched the surface of the divine destiny God wishes to explode in your life. But you must make room in your life for God to work. Take some time to reflect, and ask yourself, "Am I afraid to grow? Are there areas in my life that I need to submit to God, to make room for Him to flow?" Often, in quiet reflection, we find that we've been holding on to our life tightly. God is saying, "I have something new for you. Give me the space."

Devotional Prayer

Father, if I've shut you out from moving without restriction in my life, I repent. Help my unbelief. Help me to overcome my own limitations, so I can see your power, in Jesus' name. Amen.

180° KEYS
SCRIPTURES FOR MEDITATION

Matthew 6:33:

"But seek first his kingdom and his righteousness, and all these things will be given to you as well."

Psalm 46:10:

"He says, 'Be still, and know that I am God; I will be exalted among the nations, I will be exalted in the earth.'"

1 CHRONICLES 4:10:

"Jabez cried out to the God of Israel, "Oh, that you would bless me and enlarge my territory! Let your hand be with me, and keep me from harm so that I will be free from pain." And God granted his request."

NOTES:

You help me to walk in such a way that I can do what you want me to do. I have limited time & energy, so I need to hear you voice as I live my life.

- Nick & Michael
- Mom & Dad - health
- Chloe & Glen.
John & Jodee - health physical & emotional.

FINDING YOUR CONFIDENCE IN GOD

"Moses said to God, 'Suppose I go to the Israelites and say to them, 'The God of your fathers has sent me to you,' and they ask me, 'What is his name?' Then what shall I tell them?' God said to Moses, 'I AM WHO I AM. This is what you are to say to the Israelites: I AM has sent me to you." (Exodus 3:13-14 NIV)

When faced with a situation, task, or point in a relationship that could possibly leave us feeling vulnerable, our go-to move is often to avoid the situation all together. Why? We don't like existing in a place of uncertainty. We like to have control of the details of our lives. We often associate vulnerability with weakness. I'm sure you can remember a time when you were encouraged to do something, maybe sing that solo, give that speech, or whatever, and despite the words of support given by those around you, somewhere in the pit of your stomach you still felt an incredible sense that what was about to happen was going to blow up in your face.

You're not alone. Moses felt the same way. Imagine being told, "Hey, I want you to go down and tell Pharaoh that tomorrow over one million people are going to make their way out of your kingdom. Deal with it." Oh, by the way, if Pharaoh, or anyone, asks who sent you, tell them, "I AM did." Even after receiving definitive instruction from GOD Himself—and it doesn't get much bigger than that—Moses still had doubts. In fact, he gave God a myriad of excuses, one of them being that he had a speech impediment. God sent Aaron with Moses to function as his mouthpiece, but that didn't get Moses out of the job. God knew that Moses was the man for what was ahead. Whether Moses was ready for it or not, he left for Egypt, and had to learn that his confidence and surety for what was ahead couldn't rest on his own ability but on what God was going to do.

You see, the name I AM wasn't just a name. It was the position God took, and the decision He made. Wrapped in that name, God wasn't asking

Moses to decide whether Israel was coming out of Egypt. He wasn't asking Moses if he agreed with His plans. He was telling Moses, "Listen, I AM going to bring Israel out of Egypt. I AM about to do something in the earth." All Moses had to do was believe it. All Moses had to do was agree with what God said He was going to do.

Sometimes after God reveals His plans for us, we take it upon ourselves to try and figure out all the ins and outs. This often leaves us feeling frustrated, because we are limited and need God's direction. When God speaks to us about His plans, they are indeed that—His plans. We don't have to work out the how, why, and when. It's okay to ask those questions, but don't get caught up in that. Instead, all God asks of us is to believe in Him, to rest our confidence on Him, and He will work out the rest.

Devotional Prayer

Father, help me to rest my present and future on you. Help me not to lean on my own understanding but to rest my confidence on the greatness that you are, and on the love you continually show toward me. My future is bright! Amen.

180° KEYS
SCRIPTURES FOR MEDITATION

2 Samuel 7:28:

"Sovereign LORD, you are God! Your covenant is trustworthy, and you have promised these good things to your servant."

Psalm 13:5:

"But I trust in your unfailing love; my heart rejoices in your salvation."

Psalm 56:3:

"When I am afraid, I put my trust in you."

Romans 15:13:

"May the God of hope fill you with all joy and peace as you trust in him, so that you may overflow with hope by the power of the Holy Spirit."

NOTES:

Father help me to
trust in you in all that
I do. I desire to
walk in your way.
I call my way to trust
in you.
Fill me Lord with your
Holy Spirit and to
will trust in your way.
Help me to be fed
to your word and for
Spirit.
Amen

45

RETHINKING ISOLATION

"Be strong and courageous. Do not be afraid or terrified because of them, for the LORD your God goes with you; he will never leave you nor forsake you." (Deuteronomy 31:6)

No one wants to be alone. Society pushes the idea of companionship, that life is best experienced in the presence of a great friend, family, or spouse. I can remember my days in elementary school, where the worst placement you wanted to hold on the social ladder was that of the loner. You wanted to be popular, cool—NEVER the loner.

However, when we look at the lives of those who made significant strides in the sharing of the gospel, we see that all experienced a time of isolation. A time alone. You see, it's not so much being alone that needs to be highlighted, but rather what we learn about God, ourselves, and the world around us in times of isolation. I want to be clear. There is a difference between loneliness and isolation. The word loneliness is an ungodly construct made for one to feel that he or she is alone, with no one, seen or unseen, sharing the space. But this isn't scriptural. Jeremiah 23:23–24 (NIV) says, *"'Am I only a God nearby,' declares the Lord, 'and not a God far away? Who can hide in secret places so that I cannot see them?' declares the Lord. 'Do not I fill heaven and earth?' declares the Lord."*

Throughout Scripture, God reminds us that He is ever-present in our lives. Scripture even goes on to describe God's omnipresence through a more powerful picture in Psalm 139:8 (NIV), which says, *"If I go up to the heavens, you are there; if I make my bed in the depths, you are there."* We cannot escape His presence. He is always with us. We can feel lonely, but loneliness isn't a scriptural construct.

Taking a time of isolation from the world that exists around us is, however, scriptural. There are many examples of people in the Bible who experienced isolation. But I've discovered that God uses times of isolation for our good.

It was during times of isolation, while tending to sheep, that God prepared David and taught him principles that would later serve him as king, and bring about one of the greatest shifts in a nation's history. Isolation was training.

It was during a time of isolation that Moses received insight from God as to the direction He was going to take in delivering a nation out of slavery. Isolation brought insight.

Before Jesus started his earthly ministry, He was tempted while isolated in a desert. Isolation was preparation.

If you ever feel, perhaps, that life has left you feeling isolated and alone, don't rush to crowd your life with people, social media, your job, or anything else. Instead, keep your ears open to what God might be trying to teach you. In your place of isolation, He might be speaking to you about the greatest move on the horizon of your life. Don't fear or hate times of isolation. I promise you, God is up to something.

Devotional Prayer

Father, open my eyes to see your plan at work in my life. In times of isolation, draw me close and order my steps. Amen.

180° KEYS
SCRIPTURES FOR MEDITATION

Psalm 27:10:

"Though my father and mother forsake me, the LORD will receive me."

Isaiah 41:10:

"So do not fear, for I am with you; do not be dismayed, for I am your God. I will strengthen you and help you; I will uphold you with my righteous right hand."

Isaiah 43:2:

"When you pass through the waters, I will be with you; and when you pass through the rivers, they will not sweep over you. When you walk through the fire, you will not be burned; the flames will not set you ablaze."

Matthew 11:28:

"Come to me, all you who are weary and burdened, and I will give you rest."

NOTES:

In those times of
isolation I will see
them as a place to
get to know God
better and to begin
for Him and that
I'm not alone.
Thank you God that
You promise to be
with me wherever
I go.

50

WHAT ARE YOU SEEING?

"See, I am doing a new thing! Now it springs up;
do you not perceive it? I am making a way in
the wilderness and streams in the wasteland."
(Isaiah 43:19 NIV)

Don't judge a book by its cover. I can remember learning this principle in elementary school. The principle challenges us to never decide on the conclusion of a matter simply based on what we can see, because there is often a deeper dimension to a thing that we might be missing. Unfortunately, we live in a world that practices the total opposite. The success of a job interview should be based on your qualifications and character. However, in many cases, an employer's decision-making is influenced before you even open your mouth, simply by your outside appearance—the cover. Now, don't get me wrong. I strongly believe that we should present ourselves properly and look respectable, whether it be in a job interview or otherwise. However, I believe that more often than not, society errs on the side of judging the inside of a thing based on the outside.

Let's go a step further. The rise of social media platforms has created spaces whereby, through one post, we can present to the world the type of character, lifestyle, and status we want them to perceive us as having. Whether it's true or not is not important. That's not what is encouraged. What is pushed is to look good, look cool, look successful, because you want to get those "likes," right? You don't want to scroll through pictures of people looking "on point," and then they get to your page, and it looks below the standard. All nonsense. But it describes the pressure many face daily.

Consider, though, what God says in Isaiah 43:19. God was simply saying, "Hey, guys, I know your present situation looks a certain way, but don't make any conclusions based on your situation, based on what you can see. There is more going on behind the scenes." The verse goes a bit further, and God asks a question. *"Do you not perceive it?"* In other words, "Do you not see it?" My friends, it is possible for us to wake up day after day and totally miss the move and plan of God for our lives. Unless we take the time to stop what we're doing in life, or what I call a divine pause, and consider our lives and who holds the controls, we will forever miss what God is doing.

Our verse for today is encouraging us to look at our lives through God's eyes, and not through our own. We're limited. He's all-knowing. We don't know what tomorrow brings. God knows the end of a thing from the beginning.

When you wake up in the morning and look at yourself in the mirror, what do you see? When you get fired from your job and wonder how you're going to make ends meet, what do you see? Do you see yourself as a failure? Someone not worthy of taking another breath? No. God is saying, "Behold! I'm doing something new in your life. You may not see it right now, but I want you to see your life the way I see it."

I want to encourage you right now, in the situation you are facing, that there is something deeper going on. There is something beautiful that God is working to reveal in and through your life. See your situation, marriage, relationship, bank account, and life differently. See it through the eyes of God. He's doing something great.

Devotional Prayer

Father, Lord, open my eyes to see your hand at work in my life. Help me not to judge my life based on what I can see. Increase my faith to trust you, and my discernment to watch for your next move. I know you want the best for me. I'm excited for what you're doing in my life. Amen.

180° KEYS
SCRIPTURES FOR MEDITATION

Hebrews 11:1:

"Now faith is confidence in what we hope for and assurance about what we do not see."

Psalm 46:1:

"God is our refuge and strength, an ever-present help in trouble."

Hebrews 13:5:

"God has said, "Never will I leave you; never will I forsake you."

Psalm 33:4:

"For the word of the LORD is right and true; he is faithful in all he does."

NOTES:

THE PRINCIPLE OF EXCHANGE

"And provide for those who grieve in Zion—to bestow on them a crown of beauty instead of ashes, the oil of joy instead of mourning, and a garment of praise instead of a spirit of despair. They will be called oaks of righteousness, a planting of the LORD for the display of his splendor." (Isaiah 61:3 NIV)

I remember it as if it was yesterday. Standing in line, under the warmth of the sun, waiting. The line in front of me seemed as if it had no end. But in some way, this gave me a certain sense of safety. Eventually, I knew my time would come, the time when I would have to face the fear. The fear brought on by the Top Gun rollercoaster ride at Canada's Wonderland.

I could hear the rush of the rollercoaster above, and hear the screams of its riders. Every now and then, I'd think, "Man, if anything were to go wrong, those people would go flying across the afternoon sky." Then quickly, I would do my best to shake the thoughts. Might I also add that I wasn't alone at the amusement park. My friends stood beside me in line, oohing and aahing at the loops and turns demonstrated by the rollercoaster as it danced through the air. Despite being with my friends, however, their company offered little comfort. I was still a bit scared to go on the rollercoaster. What I remember about this was the dichotomy I felt inside. I was scared to board the rollercoaster, but at the same time I couldn't wait to go on it. I was feeling scared, but at the same time I was excited for what was ahead.

When it came my turn to board the rollercoaster, I remember summoning up the courage and deciding that I wasn't going to let this moment pass. I remember, in a way, deciding to trade in my fear for strength. Let me tell you, when it was all said and done, I ended up riding that same rollercoaster more than once. It became one of my favourite rides at the amusement park.

Whenever I think about that day, I often

think about the exchange of emotions that took place prior to boarding that ride. Making the decision to not allow fear, which at that point felt like a cloak on my back, to have the last say, and deciding that I wanted something different for my life. Making the decision to choose courage and leave behind fear. It was a decision I had to make. An exchange of perspective, outlook, and expectation.

God wants us to make the decision to exchange the rut we may find ourselves in—whether it be fear, depression, guilt, or anger—for His best for our lives. It's the principle of exchange. But guess what? He can't make the exchange for you. He provides the option, but we must make the move to accept it. The Bible encourages us by describing the work of the Lord and what He came to do in a grocery list format, all contained in our scripture verse for today. Isaiah 61:3 says *"And provide for those who grieve in Zion—to bestow on them a crown of beauty instead of ashes, the oil of joy instead of mourning, and a garment of praise instead of a spirit of despair. They will be called oaks of righteousness, a planting of the LORD for the display of his splendor."*

Songwriters went a step further, putting pen to pad to write a song that said, "Put on the garment of praise for the spirit of heaviness." I can remember singing this as a child in church. The Spirit of the Lord has come to help us put on the garment of praise in exchange for the spirit of heaviness. The Spirit of the Lord has come to do this for us, but we must accept this work in our lives. We must receive the gift of exchange that God wishes to release in our lives—joy instead of sadness, victory instead of defeat, health instead of sickness, provision instead of poverty.

My prayer for you this day is that, no matter what you may face, you will make the decision to exchange your garment. Your garment is the disposition, outlook, and perspective you have of your life and those around you. It's the disposition you possess to judge a glass as half-empty or half-full. It's the nudge inside of you that pushes you to judge missed life opportunities as either failures or learning points that will spring you forward in life, further than you've ever been before.

Exchange what is heavy on your back for God's joy, peace, and destiny. I know it may not be easy. Life can seem so heavy at times, but make the decision today; choose to centre your mind, destiny, relationships, and decisions on God's best. Make the exchange.

Devotional Prayer

Father, help me to not only see the best you have for my life, but also give me the faith and courage it takes to grab ahold of it. Help me to make the exchange. I receive the best you have for me. Amen.

180° KEYS
SCRIPTURES FOR MEDITATION

Hebrews 10:36:

"You need to persevere so that when you have done the will of God, you will receive what he has promised."

Proverbs 3:5-6:

"Trust in the LORD with all your heart and lean not on your own understanding; in all your ways submit to him, and he will make your paths straight."

Philippians 4:19:

"And my God will meet all your needs according to the riches of his glory in Christ Jesus."

Isaiah 40:29-31:

"He gives strength to the weary and increases the power of the weak. Even youths grow tired and weary, and young men stumble and fall; but those who hope in the LORD will renew their strength. They will soar on wings like eagles; they will run and not grow weary, they will walk and not be faint."

NOTES:

In Jesus I can
make an exchange,
heaviness & fear for
joy & peace.
I choose to trust in the
Lord in everything I do
so that He can do
His will in & peace
in Him.
Father, lead me by your
Holy Spirit to do
what you have called
me to do.

COMMANDING EVERY SEASON OF LIFE

"They triumphed over him by the blood of the Lamb and by the word of their testimony." (Revelation 12:11a NIV)

We're all guilty of it. When things are going well for us, we have no complaints. We speak positively, think positively, and are expecting life's situations around us to yield something positive. But if you're honest, ask yourself, "How do I act when things in my life begin to crumble?" Are you still positive? Do you still think and speak positively over your life? Or, like so many of us have done, does your self-discourse change? The Bible encourages us to not be moved by every wind of doctrine that comes our way. In fact, Ephesians 4:14 puts it like this, *"Then we will no longer be infants, tossed back and forth by the waves, and blown here and there by every wind of teaching and by the cunning and craftiness of people in their deceitful scheming."*

Doctrine speaks of the perspective or outlook on an issue. Paul is encouraging us to not be swayed by every perspective or outlook on life that a bad situation may throw at us. For example, you may experience rejection in your life, but don't let that situation define your life as a failure. Then the next day you experience breakthrough, and suddenly you believe your life definition is success. No, learn to be consistent in your outlook, despite the winds of life that may blow your way.

We learn to command our morning seasons—when things are going well in our lives. But often, when things turn sour, we throw our confession out through the window, and we begin to speak negatively over our lives. Our scripture verse for today lets us know that there are two keys that guarantee victory in the life of the believer.

The first key of victory is rooted in the finished work that Jesus did on the cross—the conquering of the works of sin and death. And through relationship with Jesus, we have access to eternal life. This eternal life is not only something that manifests when we die. No. When you make

Jesus your personal Saviour, walking in victory immediately becomes a part of your DNA. Jesus encompasses all things that pertain to life and victory. So when I received His Spirit into my life, all that He is and represents fused together with me. Now I walk through life manifesting what has already been deposited inside of me.

The second key of victory rests in my confession. Revelation 12:11 says, *"They triumphed over him by the blood of the Lamb and by the word of their testimony."* We overcome by the blood of the lamb *and* by the word of our testimony. This verse is showing us that victory also rests in our confession over our own lives. We must continually confess over our lives that which pertains to life and victory. The Bible further highlights this important victory key in Proverbs 18:21, which says, *"The tongue has the power of life and death."*

Let me give an example. It was with every stripe that Jesus received that our healing was purchased. But if we continue to speak sickness over our lives, what good will the work of Christ do? We will end up walking in sickness. The Bible encourages the poor to say, "I am rich." But if we keep decreeing poverty over our lives, then guess what? Don't expect to see increase in your bank account. When the Bible says that the power of life and death is in the tongue, we must ensure that what we confess over ourselves is in alignment with the finished work of Christ.

Are you looking for God to show up in your life? First, ask yourself, "Have I been operating the two keys of victory? Am I in step with God in relationship? How is my confession?" Often, when things are going wrong in life, we can trace the root back to the function of the two victory keys.

Devotional Prayer

Father, I thank you for your finished work on the cross. I make my confession align with your Word and destiny for my life today. I speak life, fulfilled purpose, and blessing over my life, in Jesus' name. Amen.

180° KEYS
SCRIPTURES FOR MEDITATION

Proverbs 18:21:

"The tongue has the power of life and death, and those who love it will eat its fruit."

Romans 10:9:

"If you declare with your mouth, 'Jesus is Lord,' and believe in your heart that God raised him from the dead, you will be saved."

James 1:6:

"But when you ask, you must believe and not doubt, because the one who doubts is like a wave of the sea, blown and tossed by the wind."

Mark 11:24:

"Therefore, I tell you, whatever you ask for in prayer, believe that you have received it, and it will be yours."

NOTES:

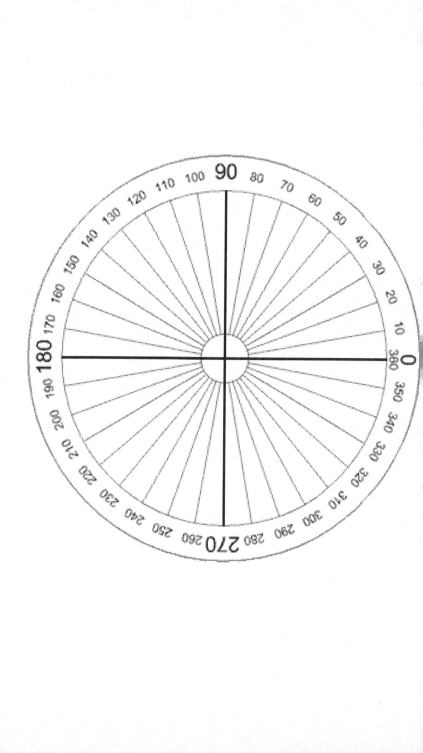

GET BACK IN THE SADDLE

"And from the days of John the Baptist until now the kingdom of heaven suffereth violence, and the violent take it by force."
(Matthew 11:12 KJV)

"We fall down, but we get up." Those are the powerful song lyrics sung by award-winning gospel artist Donnie McClurkin. This song swept through churches across North America. Soloists sang it. Dance and mime groups created movement pieces to it. It is a powerful song sung by a great artist. But the message and revelation held in the words "We fall down, but we get up" point to a greater truth that each one of us must align ourselves to follow, every day of our life.

Our focus passage for today paints the picture of a very active storyline. I've read this verse many times growing up. However, it wasn't until recently that a deeper revelation jumped out at me. Now, this verse can be unpacked in many ways, but for our purposes, in this case, when the Bible refers to the kingdom of Heaven in this scripture, it is speaking to everything that concerns the ordained plan and rule of God. Moreover, when applying it to our lives, it refers to every desire God has in His heart to establish victory in the life of humanity over the attempted resistance from the kingdom of darkness. Now, I use the term "attempted resistance" because the Bible makes it clear that the devil and his angels are already defeated. Colossians 2:15 (NKJV) says, *"And having disarmed the powers and authorities, he made a public spectacle of them, triumphing over them by the cross."*

So although the enemy may push back with resistance against the plans of God, which is the established rule of God in our lives, God's plans and desires will ultimately prevail. However, make no mistake, there is a war going on. This war isn't pretty. The Bible says, *"The kingdom of heaven suffereth violence."* Let's break this down. As I explained earlier, the kingdom of Heaven spoken about in this verse refers to the established rule of God. It refers to the rule of God in the submitted life of every believer here on Earth.

The violence spoken about can be interpreted as every situation and attack launched by the devil against your life that would work to thwart, or have you turn away or reject, the rule of God in your life. That's the violence. But check this out. There is a hidden truth many might miss when reading this verse. It's easy for us, when a negative situation occurs, to get overwhelmed and turn all our focus to the problem. Many of us point all our attention to the "violence" facing our life. But though the onslaught from the evil one may be described as ferocious, nowhere in the Bible does it tell us to shrink in fear, run for the hills, or even cry out to God. Instead, the Bible encourages us to have a clear mind, realize the intensity of the fight we are in, and with that same intensity take our life, destiny, and purpose back.

Every believer must realize that he or she is in a fight. The battle, as Scripture tells us, belongs to God. But each day there is a battle going on for your destiny, and your fight is in deciding that you will continually follow hard after God. Sometimes we fail to realize that walking out our salvation requires a strong stance of heart, soul, and mind. This stance is one that only you can take. No one else can hold the conviction to not quit but you. The devil is not going to simply let you take ahold of your divine future. He will try and fight you. He will try to keep you pressed down in the failures and perceived lost opportunities of the past, to not only keep you defeated, but to also keep you weak. It's one thing for someone to experience a momentary defeat or slip up but then get up with a renewed mind and strength, and move forward. It's another thing for one to experience defeat or a slip up and then be rendered weak, with little to nothing left to get back into the ring of life.

The devil has fought you and tried to render you weak, but no more! He has tried his hardest to slow you down and knock you off track, but no more! Maybe you've been knocked down in life. Decide to get back up, by the power of God, with even greater force than that which knocked you down, and move forward. Take back your life, your future, and your destiny. It's time to get back in the saddle.

Devotional Prayer

Father, I thank you that through you I am more

than a conqueror. I walk in victory, and my days are blessed. I walk in boldness, and I take back my destiny and declare that my life will bring glory to you. Amen.

180° KEYS
SCRIPTURES FOR MEDITATION

Psalm 27:1:

"The LORD is my light and my salvation-- whom shall I fear? The LORD is the stronghold of my life-- of whom shall I be afraid?"

Isaiah 41:13:

"For I am the LORD your God who takes hold of your right hand and says to you, Do not fear; I will help you."

James 1:12:

"Blessed is the one who perseveres under trial because, having stood the test, that person will receive the crown of life that the Lord has promised to those who love him."

Romans 8:28:

"And we know that in all things God works for the good of those who love him, who have been called according to his purpose."

NOTES:

START THINKING ABOUT WHAT YOU'RE THINKING

"We demolish arguments and every pretension that sets itself up against the knowledge of God, and we take captive every thought to make it obedient to Christ." (2 Corinthians 10:5)

Have you ever thought about how many thoughts pass through your mind each day? Researchers estimate between 50,000 to 70,000 thoughts a day for the average person. It's incredible.

When I give it more thought, I tend to wonder how many of those thoughts are negative? How many of those thoughts are, what I call, "form-making"? Form-making means once thought about, that same thought is internalized and then applied to one's character, value system, and life.

Look at it this way: Every thought that passes through your mind each day is a seed. Every seed, when watered and cared for, will spring forth and bear fruit. When you give attention to, dwell on, and rehearse negative thoughts, you water and care for those seeds. You may say, "It's not my intention." But guess what? Whether intentional or not, those seeds still get planted, watered, and cared for. The longer you dwell on those negative thoughts, the more those seeds will grow and bear fruit.

Today we see, all over the news, the manifestation of fruits that were once seeds. We read about suicides, overdoses, murders, and the list goes on. In many cases, the cause of death was the result of what was once a thought—a seed that was planted in the person's mind, watered, and cared for.

Our focus verse for today gives us direction on how we should steward the thoughts that pass through our mind. If our mind is the soil, and our thoughts are the seeds, we must become ruthless about what gets planted. Scripture uses very physical and unapologetic language regarding the stewardship of thought. It says we must demolish arguments, those perspectives that try to pose a threat to the knowledge we have about what God has for us. It doesn't stop there. It goes on to say that we must take prisoner every thought, and make it obedient to God's desire for our lives. So that means whenever a negative and defeat-filled thought passes through my mind, I must do two things. First, I must crush it; stop it right in its tracks. I don't rehearse it or dwell on it. Secondly, I must take that negative thought and confess a counter-word that aligns with the Word of God for my life. For example, a thought may pass through my mind that I will not live a victorious life. At the first inception, I stop thinking about it and speak a counter-word that aligns itself with God's report for my life. I speak Romans 8:37, which says, *"No, in all these things we are more than conquerors through him who loved us."*

My friends, it is time we get tough about what we think about. Our mind is the soil, our thoughts are the seeds. Let's ensure that we are planting that which pertains to life, destiny, and victory.

Devotional Prayer

In the name of Jesus, I take authority over the corridors of my mind. I speak that nothing shall pass that doesn't speak of life and victory. I am more than a conqueror, and my future is established, in Jesus' name. Amen.

180° KEYS
SCRIPTURES FOR MEDITATION

Romans 12:2:

"Do not conform to the pattern of this world, but be transformed by the renewing of your mind. Then you will be able to test and approve what God's will is—his good, pleasing and perfect will."

Philippians 4:8:

"Finally, brothers and sisters, whatever is true, whatever is noble, whatever is right, whatever is pure, whatever is lovely, whatever is admirable—if anything is excellent or praiseworthy—think about such things."

Matthew 15:11:

"What goes into someone's mouth does not defile them, but what comes out of their mouth, that is what defiles them."

Colossians 3:2:

"Set your minds on things above, not on earthly things."

NOTES:

_____

_____

_____

_____

_____

_____

_____

_____

_____

_____

_____

_____

_____

_____

DON'T WORRY, BE HAPPY!

"Therefore I say to you, do not worry about your life, what you will eat or what you will drink; nor about your body, what you will put on. Is not life more than food and the body more than clothing? Look at the birds of the air, for they neither sow nor reap nor gather into barns; yet your heavenly Father feeds them. Are you not of more value than they? Which of you by worrying can add one cubit to his stature? So why do you worry about clothing? Consider the lilies of the field, how they grow: they neither toil nor spin; and yet I say to you that even Solomon in all his glory was not arrayed like one of these. Now if God so clothes the grass of the field, which today is, and tomorrow is thrown into the oven, will He not much more clothe you, O you of little faith? Therefore do not worry, saying, 'What shall we eat?' or 'What shall we drink?' or 'What shall we wear?' For after all these things the Gentiles seek. For your heavenly Father knows that you need all these things." (Matthew 6:25-31)

I'm sure you can think of a time in your life when you were worried about something. That certain detail about life that kept you wide awake at night, tossing and turning. Think back to that time. Perhaps you might have been trying to figure out how the details of that situation might play out, or perhaps you were wondering what human effort you could make to turn the situation around. I have a question for you. It is a simple one. In fact, it is the same question that the Holy Spirit asked me, as I am a recovering worrier. How far did worrying about the situation get you? Did anything change? In most cases, the resounding response is no.

Worry blinds us from seeing the power and might God has to take care of us, no matter what situation we may find ourselves in. The root issue of worry is trust. We worry often because we are unsure of the outcome of a detail in life, and then we struggle to trust that things will work out. Not simply work out, but work out for our good. What I find interesting is that worry provides a false sense of security. Sometimes when we worry about something, we try to figure out things we can do, in our own power, to fix it. By doing this, we often feel as though we are moving things forward. We get a feeling that we are solving things. In reality, when we stop rehearsing different scenarios of what can be done, we are nowhere further than where we were before we started worrying in the first place. It's a false sense of security.

When we worry, it points to the strength of our faith. Not simply our faith, but our faith in God. Our focus verse makes a case using our concern about what we will eat and drink, and even asks us to consider the lilies of the field. The revelation regarding the lilies of the field and the details of their dress speaks to the numerous details of life that we, as human beings, tend to worry about. Yet we are encouraged that God, in all His power, never leaves even one lily without its glory. How much more His children—you and me?

If you find yourself in a place of worry, I want to ask you the same question asked in the Bible. *"If God so clothes the grass of the field, which today is, and tomorrow is thrown into the oven, will He not much more clothe you, O you of little faith?"* My dear friend, trust that the God of the universe is making a way on your behalf. Worry only limits your ability to see God work. When we trust God that He is working it out, we can find room within ourselves to experience joy and peace. You can't find peace and joy in the midst of a storm if you're too busy rehearsing the situation and everything negative about it. You must drop worry so that, through faith, God can send His peace that passes all understanding into your situation, peace that will guard your heart and your mind. Sit back, relax, and watch God make a way in your life. It's not over. God's got you. Don't worry, be happy.

Devotional Prayer

Father, I trust you this day with my life. I will not worry, doubt, or fear. Operating that way is a thing of the past. I decree this day that my life is safe and secure with you. Amen.

180° KEYS
SCRIPTURES FOR MEDITATION

Philippians 4:6-7:

"Do not be anxious about anything, but in every situation, by prayer and petition, with thanksgiving, present your requests to God. And the peace of God, which transcends all understanding, will guard your hearts and your minds in Christ Jesus."

Matthew 11:28-30:

"Come to me, all you who are weary and burdened, and I will give you rest. Take my yoke upon you and learn from me, for I am gentle and humble in heart, and you will find rest for your souls. For my yoke is easy and my burden is light."

Colossians 3:15:

"Let the peace of Christ rule in your hearts, since as members of one body you were called to peace. And be thankful."

2 Thessalonians 3:16:

"Now may the Lord of peace himself give you peace at all times and in every way. The Lord be with all of you."

NOTES:

CONFESSION AND ME

"Shadrach, Meshach and Abednego replied to him, "King Nebuchadnezzar, we do not need to defend ourselves before you in this matter. If we are thrown into the blazing furnace, the God we serve is able to deliver us from it, and he will deliver us from Your Majesty's hand."
(Daniel 3:16-17)

Shadrach, Meshach, and Abednego—the three Hebrew boys. Their story is one of the first biblical stories taught to children in Sunday school classrooms, everywhere. I remember learning about them as a child. I don't know what it was about the story that made it stick in my memory. Maybe it was the perfect balance of good versus evil, and good winning in the most dramatic of ways. Perhaps it was the courage they displayed in the face of what many would conclude to be certain death that stood out to me. I'm not sure. But one thing I can say that gripped me as a child after hearing this story was that if you believe and have faith, there is no situation too great that God will not see you through. Simple lesson, right?

Not long ago, I revisited the story of the three Hebrew boys, and got to thinking. Where did these three men get the courage to believe in God so steadfastly? I understand that they believed in God, literally in the face of fire, but how were they able to tap into such an unmovable faith? Then it hit me. The secret is hidden in verses 16 and 17 of our passage. *"Shadrach, Meshach and Abednego replied to him, 'King Nebuchadnezzar, we do not need to defend ourselves before you in this matter. If we are thrown into the blazing furnace, the God we serve is able to deliver us from it, and he will deliver us from Your Majesty's hand.'"*

Did you miss it? Their unmovable faith was strengthened and brought to life by their confession. Let me tell you this, by the confession of the three Hebrew boys, as far as they were concerned, God had already delivered them from the fiery furnace and from anything else King Nebuchadnezzar might have had up his sleeve. The Bible teaches us that life and death are in the power of the tongue (Proverbs 18:21). That means that what we speak, we give life to, which also means that by the confession of our mouths, we have the power to create our own destiny and, by extension, the world we live in. The three Hebrew boys, by the power of confession, spoke to their destiny concerning the situation they were in, and spoke life. When confession and faith in God meet, it is a powerful thing.

When you encounter an unfavourable situation, when life gets hard, when you experience a tough break, what is your confession? I'm asking specifically about your confession. I believe that your confession can be more important than your level of faith. If I have faith in God, but the confession of my mouth speaks defeat, how can I expect to see life out of my situation? Your confession must match your faith. So I ask you again, what have you been speaking? I want to encourage you, no matter how insurmountable your situation may seem, no matter how uncertain the future may appear, trust God that He *will* see you through, and then let the confession of your mouth speak victory, life, and a successful end.

Devotional Prayer

In the name of Jesus, I speak that I am the head and not the tail. Above only and never beneath. I decree that I am blessed in my going out and in my coming in. Everything I put my hands to do prospers. Every day I wake, I decree that I walk in victory and blessing. Amen.

180° KEYS
SCRIPTURES FOR MEDITATION

1 Corinthians 15:57:

"But thanks be to God! He gives us the victory through our Lord Jesus Christ."

1 John 5:4:

"For everyone born of God overcomes the world. This is the victory that has overcome the world, even our faith."

Romans 8:37:

"No, in all these things we are more than conquerors through him who loved us."

Psalm 3:3:

"But you, Lord, are a shield around me, my glory, the One who lifts my head high."

NOTES:

GOD VERSUS YOUR OWN STRENGTH

"In their hearts humans plan their course, but the LORD establishes their steps."
(Proverbs 16:9)

How many times have you been faced with a situation in life that you tried to fix alone? I mean, a situation where you knew deep down in your heart, "I need to turn this over to God." But for some reason, as we all so often do, you decided to take it into your own hands. How did things go? Did you get the full desired end you were hoping for? In most cases, if you are honest with yourself, you didn't. The truth of the matter is that when we decide to address the situations life throws at us on our own, more often than not, we lose.

Present-day culture teaches us that we need to face the world and make things happen on our own. Think about it. Some of today's most popular brands and cultural thought push a mindset that does not encourage a reliance on something greater than us. We have cultural thoughts and brands that push ideas like "Be your own boss." Don't get me wrong, I get the essence of what companies are trying to promote. But I also realize that when we are consistently bombarded with messages that push self-reliance to achieve, the potency of relying on God as the only way-maker in life becomes diluted.

Much to the opposite of present-day culture, we don't have a full perspective of our life. You might be asking, "Sheldon, how do you know this to be true?" I'll prove it to you, my dear friend. There is only one being who is omniscient and omnipresent. Isaiah 46:10 puts it this way, *"I make known the end from the beginning, from ancient times, what is still to come. I say, 'My purpose will stand, and I will do all that I please."*

God knows the beginning and end of every matter that concerns us. What an advantage. Oftentimes, when we decide to face life situations on our own, we only have one vantage point, and that is our own. We make decisions based on what we think is the right move. But we don't have full certainty of how all parties involved will feel, how the situation will end, if certain changing conditions will arise, or what the full, lasting result will be. Only God himself has the insight to know the end from the beginning of a thing. He is the only person who knows the end of your life from its beginning. What insight. It's amazing.

Why wouldn't you want Him in your corner, to lean on? To seek wisdom and insight as you walk through life. Don't get me wrong, I'm not trying to suggest that you live a life where you are afraid of making every decision, like whether to wear the green shirt or the red one to work in the morning. No, no. But I am saying that if we are honest with ourselves, sometimes we tend to run ahead of God and not include Him in the decisions and paths we take in life, not realizing that when we do so it's like walking blindfolded.

So what is the healthy balance? I believe that it is in our scriptural passage for today. We make the plans, but God orders our steps. The verse is saying that it's okay to make plans for your life, but understand that they must be balanced with you first submitting and finding out God's plan for your life. He wants the best for you.

God is not there to hold you back. God is there because He wants to have a relationship with you, so that you can see the path ahead of you. Don't live your life blindfolded.

Devotional Prayer

Father, this day I submit my life holistically to you. I submit to your guidance, leadership, and lordship in my life, knowing you have the best continually planned for my life. Amen.

180° KEYS
SCRIPTURES FOR MEDITATION

Psalm 143:10:

"Teach me to do your will, for you are my God; may your good Spirit lead me on level ground."

1 Peter 5:6:

"Humble yourselves, therefore, under God's mighty hand, that he may lift you up in due time."

Psalm 119:133:

"Direct my footsteps according to your word; let no sin rule over me."

James 4:7:

"Submit yourselves, then, to God. Resist the devil, and he will flee from you."

NOTES:

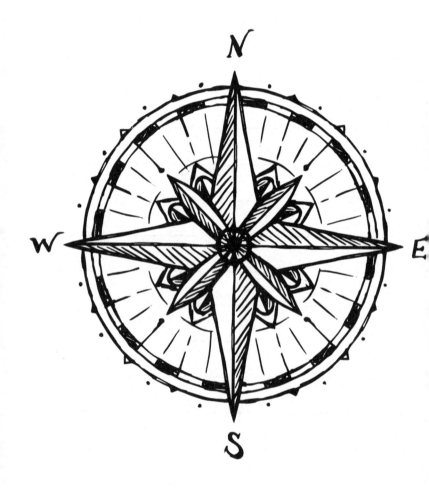

HOPE FOR THE HOPELESS

"Cast all your anxiety on him because he cares for you." (1 Peter 5:7)

We live busy lives. The older we get, the more the demands of life grow and become progressively more severe. The commitments of days past, like completing homework or that science fair project that weighed so heavily on many of us as children in elementary school, pale in comparison to the demands of life as an adult. More so, when children are added to the list. In short, life can pull on you. For many, over time, this can bring about a sense of inadequacy and hopelessness. Thoughts like, "How will I get this done? What about this bill payment? Will I have enough time to finish this?" begin to swirl in the mind.

Hopelessness. It's a terrible state to find yourself living in. You feel alone, powerless, and trapped, as though there's no way out. But hear me when I tell you that feeling of hopelessness is a trap of the enemy. I will tell you why. The goal of the enemy, in making you feel hopeless, is primarily to make you feel as if no one cares about the situation you are in. When we feel hopeless, mixed into that emotion is the feeling that if we could just get some help, which is really saying if we could just get someone to care about what we're going through, all would be well. When we operate and live in a state of feeling hopeless, we often make rash and unwise decisions to turn the tide of the situation. Living from a place of hopelessness creates a sense of desperation, over time. All of this is rooted in a false report—that no one cares about what you are going through.

However, our verse for today encourages us and reminds us to cast all our anxiety and cares of life on God, for He cares for us. First, the scripture invites us to cast our cares. This literally means to throw. If you've ever thrown anything in your life—a football or baseball—you know it takes some sort of effort. I believe nothing written in God's Word is by accident. This verse is directing us, while also being sensitive to the human experience. It says to "cast," presupposing that it is going to take some effort on our part. It's so easy for us to take upon ourselves the cares of life, but the scripture is saying, with every effort you have, throw those cares on God. Get the strength, no matter how hard it may be, how severe life's demands may be, and throw those cares on God.

I have good news for you. It doesn't end there. The verse goes on to tell us to throw our cares on God, because He cares for us. He's in our corner. We're not alone. We can rest secure in throwing our cares on God, because He wishes the best for us. He's here to carry you through this, so you don't have to feel hopeless. You, indeed, have a hope. That hope rests in the God of the universe, whose greatest love is looking back at you each morning in the mirror. If you are feeling at the end of your rope, don't throw in the towel. Throw your cares on Him. God is here, and He cares. There is hope for the hopeless.

Devotional Prayer

Father, this day I cast all my cares, concerns, and fears on you. I believe that, in your hands, all is well that concerns me. I receive the peace only you can give this day concerning life situations, and thank you for victory through it all. Amen.

180° KEYS
SCRIPTURES FOR MEDITATION

Job 11:18-19:

"You will be secure, because there is hope; you will look about you and take your rest in safety."

Psalm 147:11:

"The LORD delights in those who fear him, who put their hope in his unfailing love."

1 Corinthians 2:9:

"However, as it is written: 'What no eye has seen, what no ear has heard, and what no human mind has conceived'— the things God has prepared for those who love him."

Jeremiah 29:11:

"For I know the plans I have for you,' declares the LORD, 'plans to prosper you and not to harm you, plans to give you hope and a future."

NOTES:

DON'T LET IT SHAKE YOU!

"You will keep in perfect peace those whose minds are steadfast, because they trust in you." (Isaiah 26:3)

Have you ever tried your hand at something, and failed? Maybe you were unsure if you could make the basketball team or track team, but despite your feelings, you stuck your neck out in faith, believed in yourself, and tried. How did you feel when things didn't work out? Did you feel like throwing in the towel and never trying again? Was your faith shattered? Don't be tough on yourself; so many of us have been there. For some, it might not be trying out for a sports team. It might be gaining the courage to speak in front of a crowd, or to walk into a job interview.

The most important thing to remember is that no matter how *changing* life circumstances may be, we must be *unchanging* in our view of them. We must believe that we have a God who is going to see us through any situation that may come our way.

Let's go a step further. The Bible is very clear in identifying the endgame of the enemy we face. Just to be clear, the enemy I'm referring to is the devil. John 10:10 says, *"The thief comes only to steal and kill and destroy."* The thief being referred to here is the devil. No matter what the enemy may seek to plot against you, the endgame is to achieve one, or all three, of these results: steal, kill, and destroy. Harsh, you say? Well, it is true.

The goal of the devil is to steal, kill, and destroy every bit of God-given destiny and blessing ordained for your life. How does he achieve that? By orchestrating life situations that will shake your faith. Not just your faith, but your faith in God. Why? Because faith is the lifeline to one's relationship with God. Faith is the seed that springs forth when we make Christ the Lord of our life, believing that there is no other way we can live but in the arms of a risen King.

Faith is a key to pleasing God. Hebrews 11:6 says, *"And without faith it is impossible to please God, because anyone who comes to him must believe that he exists and that he rewards those who earnestly seek him."* But if the enemy can shake our faith, we are cut off from our life source, which is God. When our faith is shaken, our prayer life is affected. We quickly lose the desire to pray, because who would want to speak to someone they have no, or little, faith in?

The life circumstances that the enemy throws at you are designed to shake your faith. Our verse for today encourages us that peace, in the middle of the storms of life, goes to the person who does not allow his or her faith to be shaken.

Notice that the scripture is not bound by time. It does not say that peace is for those who are steadfast, before or during or even after a point. The scripture is final and continuous in its state. It says that peace is given to the person whose mind is, and who lives, in a place of being steadfast. Why? Because their faith continues to be rooted in God. Their faith is rooted in God's ability.

The peace we are searching for in life, especially when we may feel most inadequate, rests in our decision to keep our mind unmoved and rooted, not in our own strength, but in something greater than us—God.

Some of you have been living a life full of

turmoil and stress. Could the reason be that you've been putting too much of your mind's focus, and your faith, on yourself and the situation, and not enough on God? From this day forward, no matter the storm, practice to not change your mind. Resolve in yourself to keep the faith.

Declarative Prayer

In the name of Jesus, I decree and declare that I will be steadfast in my faith and hope in Christ. I will not be shaken or tossed in every direction by whatever life may throw at me. I decree that I have unshakable faith, unmovable hope, and unchanging focus on God's saving work in my life. Amen.

180° KEYS
SCRIPTURES FOR MEDITATION

Psalm 62:6:

"Truly he is my rock and my salvation; he is my fortress, I will not be shaken."

Psalm 16:8:

"I keep my eyes always on the LORD. With him at my right hand, I will not be shaken."

Psalm 125:1:

"Those who trust in the LORD are like Mount Zion, which cannot be shaken but endures forever."

NOTES:

MAYBE IT'S TIME TO GET A NEW CREW

"Do not be deceived: evil company corrupts good habits" (1 Corinthians 15:33)

There is a popular phrase that I heard while growing up as a child—"Birds of a feather flock together." The basic premise is that people who are likeminded in their perspective of the world around them often keep company together. Now, as a child, I didn't totally see and weigh the validity of the principle, but fast-forward a couple of decades, and I've learned and witnessed that this principle holds some truth. What I find interesting is the power of human agency tucked away in this principle. It shows that people rally, and often in great numbers, around common interests, passions, and desires. The effects of this can either develop into something positive or negative; it depends on the people involved. But the principle still stands true. When analyzing the most powerful movements that have shaped culture and society in history, we can find the root in people who shared common perspective coming together to bring about change. For example, this can be seen in civil rights marches during the late 60s and 70s against racism. People came together, believing that racism and segregation must stop. Thus, it further strengthened a common voice for change in how we view each other as human beings.

1 Corinthians 15:33 highlights the "bird of a feather" concept for us in a much deeper light. It warns us to choose our company carefully. We will end up picking up the habits of the people we form relationships with. This includes their outlook on life, their beliefs, and their values. It *will* rub off on you. There is no escaping it. If you think back to your days in high school, the lesson of choosing your company carefully is even easier to understand. I can remember individuals in high school who started hanging out with certain groups of people and, over time, they succumbed to the direction of the group. Oftentimes, it carried along with it unfortunate results.

Sometimes we think hanging around certain people or groups won't affect us, but do you act the same in every scenario? Of course not. Now, don't get me wrong, I know sometimes we carry ourselves differently, depending on the circumstances we find ourselves in. But we're not talking about that. I'm talking about the groups of people we decide to form relationships with. Every time you form a friendship with someone, there is an unseen, and somewhat subconscious, agreement that takes place. You both decide to let your natural guard down to a degree, to get to know each other. You let them in. You expose yourself. And this can be a healthy thing. 1 Corinthians 15:33 is not pushing us away from connection or friendship, but rather saying to be watchful as to who we let in, because they will influence our development.

As we continue to pursue the purpose God has for our lives, let's practice to be mindful of who we are letting into our lives. Let us choose people who can push us further down the path towards God's perfection. Let's practice to create agreements with people who can sharpen us. Proverbs 27:17 puts it this way, *"As iron sharpens iron, so one person sharpens another."* We want to be in friendships that sharpen us, and not make us dull. If you find yourself constantly making the wrong decisions and going down a path that you know is not God's best for you, firstly take responsibility for your own actions and make the necessary adjustments. Secondly, look at the company you keep. It may be time to get a new crew.

Devotional Prayer

Father, order my steps and lead me to choose relationships with likeminded people who will help to push me towards the destiny you have for my life. Amen.

180° KEYS
SCRIPTURES FOR MEDITATION

Proverbs 12:26:

"The righteous choose their friends carefully, but the way of the wicked leads them astray."

Proverbs 13:20:

"Walk with the wise and become wise, for a companion of fools suffers harm."

Proverbs 27:17:

"As iron sharpens iron, so one person sharpens another."

Psalm 1:1:

"Blessed is the one who does not walk in step with the wicked or stand in the way that sinners take or sit in the company of mockers."

NOTES:

YOUR NEXT LEVEL IS WAITING ON YOU

"For we must all appear before the judgment seat of Christ, so that each of us may receive what is due us for the things done while in the body, whether good or bad." (2 Corinthians 5:10)

Life is filled with ups and downs. It's filled with changing circumstances, some of which we can plan for, while others come to surprise us. With the ever-changing nature of life experiences, if we are not careful, we can find ourselves placing the blame for where we are in life, what we've accomplished, why we didn't get the promotion, or why we were passed over at work, on just that, life circumstances, and not on ourselves. In short, we blame people and circumstances for where we are in life, instead of taking responsibility for it ourselves.

Let's take it a step further. If we're not careful,

sometimes we find ourselves blaming God for things that haven't happened in our lives, when if we're honest with ourselves, He has been asking us to make certain adjustments to better position ourselves for the next level of blessing. But because His request seemed like an inconvenience to us, we didn't bother to do it. I want to let you know a hard truth about life. It's something that I've come to understand, and it took a while to sink in. You are EXACTLY where you are in life because you've chosen to be there. Sit with that for a moment. Now, before you take any bit of offence to it, think about how empowering that truth is.

If you are where you are in life because you've chosen to be there, the greater truth is that you can CHANGE where you are in life, too. Too many of us blame life circumstances or other people for the place—socio-economic, job, or even church—we find ourselves in.

Why is it easy to blame other factors? The answer is simple. When we blame others, it puts the pressure on everything and everyone around us to change, except us. We want other things or people to do the heavy lifting. Taking responsibility means you are assuming the driver's seat, under God's leading, of course. But many people aren't ready to assume that level of responsibility over their life. It takes guts, it takes maturity, and it takes effort.

We, as humans, are pre-programmed to sustain levels of comfort in life. We often say we want change, but most people would rather stay in their comfort zone. I want you to know that the moment you choose to put your life in cruise control, you are also saying yes to the consequences that come along with that. 2 Corinthians 5:10 puts the spotlight on us, as people. The scriptural context is speaking of the judgment everyone must, and will, face someday. But I believe the principle it teaches has a universal lesson: you must take responsibility for your life—its direction, its potency, and its development. The ball is in no one else's court but your own.

Devotional Prayer

Father, this day I take ownership of, and responsibility for, my life and its direction. I no longer blame others or life's situations for the lost opportunities you've offered me that I refused to take. I step up to the plate, and with your direction, I move forward in maturity, in Jesus' name. Amen.

180° KEYS
SCRIPTURES FOR MEDITATION

Colossians 2:6-7:

"So then, just as you received Christ Jesus as Lord, continue to live your lives in him, rooted and built up in him, strengthened in the faith as you were taught, and overflowing with thankfulness."

Ephesians 4:14:

"Then we will no longer be infants, tossed back and forth by the waves, and blown here and there by every wind of teaching and by the cunning and craftiness of people in their deceitful scheming."

2 Peter 3:17-18:

"Therefore, dear friends, since you have been forewarned, be on your guard so that you may not be carried away by the error of the lawless and fall from your secure position. But grow in

the grace and knowledge of our Lord and Savior Jesus Christ. To him be glory both now and forever! Amen."

1 Corinthians 7:1:

"Therefore, since we have these promises, dear friends, let us purify ourselves from everything that contaminates body and spirit, perfecting holiness out of reverence for God."

NOTES: